A

NATIONAL STRENGTH AND
INTERNATIONAL DUTY

THE STAFFORD LITTLE LECTURES
FOR 1917

The Stafford Little Lectures

The Independence of the Executive
By GROVER CLEVELAND

The Government in the Chicago Strike
By GROVER CLEVELAND

The Venezuelan Boundary Controversy
By GROVER CLEVELAND

Government of the Canal Zone
By GEORGE W. GOETHALS

The Two Hague Conferences
By JOSEPH H. CHOATE

Experiments in Government and the Essentials
of the Constitution
By ELIHU ROOT

The Balkan Wars
By JACOB GOULD SCHURMAN

National Strength and International Duty
By THEODORE ROOSEVELT

Each $1.00 net, by mail $1.06

NATIONAL STRENGTH AND INTERNATIONAL DUTY

BY

THEODORE ROOSEVELT

PRINCETON UNIVERSITY PRESS
PRINCETON
LONDON: HUMPHREY MILFORD
OXFORD UNIVERSITY PRESS
1917

NATIONAL STRENGTH AND INTERNATIONAL DUTY

Before dealing with the proper subject matter of the lecture, I wish to take up —and brush aside—the objection to truth-telling glibly urged by some extremely partisan papers, and by some very silly persons, who condemn all criticism of our shortcomings on the pretence that "criticism tends to weaken the Government and is therefore disloyal." The well meaning persons who are misled by this shallow pretence would do well to ponder the fact that this is the position which, in reference to me, has been heatedly upheld by the Hearst papers, and by German-American papers like the Staats Zeitung, which in this war have served Germany by justify-

8688

ing her actions, by enthusiastically hailing all peace proposals which would leave her mistress of the international situation, and by assailing our Allies, especially England. The pro-Germans clamor for an indecisive peace, covertly back Germany or oppose our Allies, or seek to interfere with all proposals to make us genuinely efficient in the war, and by their utterances to rouse and increase discontent with the war; and then they curry favor with the foolish, at the same time that they continue to serve their real purposes, by denouncing those who seek to make us more effective in the war by honestly endeavoring to eliminate the things that make us ineffective. The fact that the pro-Germans, with ostentatious sham loyalty, denounce honest criticism of our faults ought to convince all honest persons who are also intelligent that such criticism at this time is vitally necessary. Such criticism, to be of use, must be made in the living present, and not after the event, and only of the dead past. Let these persons read Washington's unsparing criticisms of, and to, the Continental Congress; let them read Lincoln's merciless criticisms of Pierce and Buchanan; and they will understand that honest and truthful and fearless criticism of grave shortcomings may be absolutely indispensable in order to secure triumph in a grave crisis.

Any man who preaches to others should rightly be required to show that he has himself, according to his power, acted upon the doctrines he preaches and that he has not lightly changed them or lightly adopted them. Moreover, any public man who criticizes shortcomings in the present should rightly be required to show that he has criticized similar shortcomings in the past, and that he has himself when in power endeavored to do that which he now holds that others ought to do or to have done. For this reason I make the following quotations from my writings in the past.

In the life of Thomas Hart Benton, written thirty-one years ago, I put my position as follows:

"After all this ruffianism was really not a whit worse in its effect upon the national character than was the case with certain of the Universal Peace and Non-Resistance developments in the Northeastern States; in fact, it was more healthy. A class of professional non-combatants is as hurtful to the real healthy growth of a nation as is a class of fire-eaters; for a weakness or folly is nationally as bad as a vice or worse and in the long run a [professional pacifist] may be quite as undesirable a citizen as is a duelist. No man who is not willing to bear arms and to fight for his rights can give a good reason why he should be entitled to the privilege of living in a free community."

What I thus said thirty-one years ago I am saying now, and it is the doctrine which I have preached ever since. It has been the burden of my talk for preparedness during the last three years and a quarter. In the concluding sentence I foreshadowed the doctrine that Universal Service and Universal Suffrage should go hand in hand, because no man is fit to vote in a country if he is not willing to fight for it.

Foolish creatures object to my calling attention to our gross shortcomings and failures at this time—our failure to prepare in advance, our failure to provide airplanes, our failure to provide proper rifles and cannon, proper equipment, proper gas masks, warm clothing for our troops in the training camps. The following extracts, written about the Administration of which I was a part, at the time when I was Assistant Secretary of the

Navy, and Colonel in the Army; and written in reference to my own party, and to the Administration which I was shortly to join, when I was Governor of the State of New York: will show that I then took precisely the position that I take now. According to my belief it is the only wise and patriotic position, the only position that a self-respecting American, who knows the facts, has any business to take.

Before the Naval War College, in June 1897, when I was Assistant Secretary of the Navy, I made an address in which I spoke, in part, as follows:

"Arbitration is an excellent thing. But ultimately those who wish to see this country at peace with foreign nations will be wise if they place reliance upon a first class fleet of first class battleships rather than on any arbitration treaty which the wit of man can devise. Cowardice in a race, as in an individual, is the unpardonable sin, *and a wilful failure to prepare for danger may, in its effects, be as bad as cowardice.* The timid man who cannot fight, and the selfish, shortsighted or foolish man who will not take the steps that will enable him to fight, stand on almost the same plane. The nation must have physical, no less than moral courage; the capacity to do and dare and die at need, and that grim and steadfast resolution which alone will carry a great people through a great peril. Unreadiness for war is merely rendered more disastrous by readiness to bluster. *It has always been true, and in this age it is more than ever true that it is too late to prepare for war when the time for peace has passed. It is too late to make ready for war when the fight has once begun.* The preparation must come before that. Diplomacy is utterly useless when there is no force behind it; the diplomat is the servant, not the master, of the soldier. If, in the future, we have war, it will almost certainly come because of some action, or lack of action, on our part in the way of refusing to accept responsibilities at the proper time, or failing to prepare for war when war does not threaten. An ignoble peace is even worse than an unsuccessful war. We ask for an armament fit for the nation's needs, not primarily to fight but to avoid fighting. Peace, like freedom, is not a gift that tarries long in the hands of cowards or of those too feeble or too short-sighted to deserve it, and we ask to be given the means to insure that honorable peace which alone is worth having."

In this and in the subsequent quotations I condense, for the sake of space, by omitting sentences and parts of sentences, but without changing a word which would change the sense. I call especial attention to the sentences I have italicised in this address made over twenty-one years ago. At the same time, in a book entitled "Naval Operations" of the War of 1812, I said:

"Each [of the two main combatants in the war] inclined to view with suspicion the neutral who made a cold blooded profit out of the sufferings of both, . . . there was but one possible way to gain or keep the respect of either, and that was by the possession of power and the readiness to use it if necessary. There never was a better example of the ultimate evil caused by a timid effort to secure peace through the sacrifice of honor and the refusal to make preparations for war . . . [and to] find some patent substitute for war. Contempt is the emotion of all others which a nation should be least willing to arouse. . . . lack of preparation, laxness of organization, invite disasters which can be but partially repaired. [Other things being equal] victory in any contest will go to the man or the nation that has earned it by thorough preparation."

As Colonel of the First Volunteer Cavalry, September 10, 1898, I notified the Secretary of War, my official superior, as to conditions during the campaign, doing this in answer to a circular issued by Commander Major General Shafter. I set down the exact facts, good and bad; I described the confusion and the good fighting both alike. The rifles and ammunition were excellent and were well handled; items in the food supply, such as the corn beef, were excellent. I reported "the canned roast beef as worse than a failure as part of the rations, and the effort to eat it made some of the men sick." I further reported that:

"On the return trip the rations were short, the water very bad and the lack of ice for the weak and sickly men was very much felt. During the month following the landing of the Army in Cuba the food supplies were generally short in quantity. The hardtack was often moldy, the bacon was usually good. Members of the Illinois Regiment at one time offered our men a dollar apiece for hardtacks. I wish to bear testimony to the energy and capacity of Colonel Weston, the Commissary General with the Expedition: As regards the clothing, the blue shirts were excellent, the leggings were good, the shoes were very good, the undershirts not very good, the drawers bad and the trousers poor. Just before leaving Cuba most of the men were in tatters, some being actually bare-footed while others were in rags or partly dressed in clothes captured from the Spaniards. The conditions in the big hospitals in the rear were frightful, beyond description, from lack of supplies, lack of medicine, lack of doctors, nurses and attendants, and especially from lack of transportation. The wounded and sick who were sent back suffered so much that finally we never sent any to the rear save in the direst need."

These comments were made to my superior officers when I was in the Army and just prior to my being nominated as Governor of New York. I pointed out the grave faults in our Administration then, not to embarrass the Government, of which I was a hearty supporter, but because it was a plain duty to the country to act precisely as I acted. Exactly the same reasons influence me now, when I point out that broom sticks are insufficient substitutes for rifles, or that eight men drilled with one rifle, without any ammunition, will not learn the work of soldiering as rapidly as if each had his own modern rifle, or when I say that in bitter November weather a soldier without an overcoat and in a cotton uniform and summer underclothing and socks is not sufficiently clad. Unless our people thoroughly and vividly understand the evil results of failure to prepare in advance, it may be set down as certain that they never will prepare in advance.

While Governor of New York, in November 1899, the year before I myself ran as candidate for Vice-President, I made an earnest plea for preparedness in advance and set forth absolutely without equivocation the shortcomings of the Army at the time of the Santiago Campaign. I said in part (again I condense, as in most of these quotations):

"The Artillery had for thirty-five years had no field practice that was in the slightest degree adequate to its needs. The bureaus in Washington were absolutely enmeshed in red tape and were held, for the most part, by elderly men of fine records in the past who were no longer fit to break through routine and to show the extraordinary energy, business capacity, initiative and willingness to accept responsibility which were needed. The Santiago campaign was a welter of confusion with utter lack of organization and of that skilled leadership which can come only through practice. The Army was more than once uncomfortably near disaster, from which it was saved by the remarkable fighting qualities of its individual fractions, and above all by the incompetency of its foes. To go against a well organized, well handled, well led foreign foe under such conditions would inevitably have meant failure and humiliation. It will be impossible to get good results in war if the nation, through its representatives, has failed to make adequate provision for a proper Army and to provide for the reorganization of the Army and for its practice in time of peace."

I was writing of my own party, and of what occurred under the Administration of which I was part. I then declined to suppress or alter the truth; and those critics of mine are indeed foolish who believe that I can be frightened into at this time refusing to speak that minimum portion of the truth which it is imperative on behalf of the nation now to set forth.

In my Autobiography I christened my chapter on the Spanish war, "The War of America The Unready." Writing in 1913, I said:

"There is no more utterly useless and even utterly mischievous citizen, than the peace-at-any-price, universal arbitration type of being, who is always complaining, either about war or else about the cost of the armaments which act as the insurance against war. In the present stage of civilization a proper armament is the surest guarantee of peace and is the only guarantee that war, if it does come, will not mean irreparable and overwhelming disaster. The huckster or pawn-broker type is usually physically timid and likes to cover an unworthy fear of the most just war under high sounding names. The large mollycoddle vote . . . consists of the people who are soft physically and morally or who have a twist in them which makes them cantankerous and unpleasant as long as they can be so with safety to their bodies. In addition there are the good people with no imagination and no foresight who think war will not come, but that if it does come, Armies and Navies can be improvised. I abhor unjust war; I believe that war should never be resorted to when or so long as it is honorably possible to avoid it. I advocate preparation for war in order to avert war, and I should never advocate war unless it were the only alternative to dishonor. I describe the folly of which so many of our people were formerly guilty, in order that we may in our own day be on our guard against similar folly."

I call especial attention to the last sentence. I was speaking of the Administration and of the party organization in which I had held a position of some prominence. My motives in so speaking were precisely the same as my motives in describing the folly of which we have been guilty during the last three years and a quarter. I wish that any persons who believe that I have in any fundamental way changed my attitude would read the final chapter in my Autobiography, "The Peace of Righteousness." Every position I have taken during the past three and one quarter years is foreshadowed, often in absolute detail, by what I said in that chapter.

As President I, many scores of times, took precisely the position I now take. I quote almost at random. In 1901, in my message to Congress, I said:

"We desire the peace which comes as of right to the just man armed, not the

peace granted on terms of ignominy, to
the craven and the weakling. It is not
possible to improvise [military force]
after war breaks out. If we fail to show
forethought and preparation now, there
may come a time when disaster will befall
us instead of triumph. There is no surer
way of courting national disaster than to
be opulent, aggressive and unarmed.
Only by actual handling and providing
for men in masses while they are marching, camping, embarking and disembark-
ing will it be possible to train the higher
officers to perform their duties well and
smoothly. It is utterly impossible in the
excitement and haste of impending war
[to work] satisfactorily if the arrange-
ments have not been made long before-
hand."

In December 1905, in my message to
Congress, I said:

"We can do nothing of permanent
value for peace unless we keep ever clearly
in mind the ethical element which lies at
the root of the problem. Our aim is righteousness. When peace and righteousness

conflict then a great and upright people can never for a moment hesitate to follow the path which leads toward righteousness, even though that path also leads toward war. We have scant sympathy with the sentimentalist who dreads oppression less than physical suffering, and who would prefer a shameful peace to the pain and toil sometimes lamentably necessary in order to secure a righteous peace. As the world is now, only that nation is equipped for peace that knows how to fight and that will not shrink from fighting if ever the conditions become such that war is demanded in the name of the highest morality. We cannot consider the question of our foreign policy without at the same time treating of the Army and Navy. Only by training in advance can we be sure that in actual war, field operations and those at sea will be carried on successfully."

I dwelt upon our duties about peace and war and the duty of preparedness again and again, in message after message. In my message to Congress in December 1906, for example, I said:

"A just war is in the long run far better for a nation's soul than the most prosperous peace obtained by acquiescence in wrong or in injustice."

Then in advocating preparedness I said:

"It is earnestly to be wished that we would profit by the teaching of history in this matter. A strong and wise people will study its own failures no less than its triumphs, for there is wisdom to be learned from the study of both, of the mistake as well as of the success. For this purpose nothing can be more instructive than a rational study of the War of 1812. During the preceding twelve years our people refused to make any preparations whatever regarding the Army or the Navy. They saved a million or two of dollars by so doing, and in mere money paid a hundredfold for each million they thus saved during a war which brought untold suffering and which resulted merely in what was, in effect, a drawn battle. The little Republic of Switzerland sets us an excellent example

in all matters connected with building up
an efficient citizen soldiery."

I was not then acquainted with the term
"universal obligatory military training";
hardly any American was; but I knew of
the *thing,* although not the *term;* and I
held up Switzerland as a model to us, in
pursuance of the doctrine I was preach-
ing, that no freeman had a right to live in
a free nation if he would not bear arms,
and therefore train himself to bear arms
efficiently, in the nation's service.

In my message to Congress of December 1907, I said:

"Again and again we have suffered because there has not been sufficient preparation in advance for possible war. As
a nation we have always been short-
sighted in providing for the efficiency of
the Army in time of peace. Declamation
against militarism has no more serious
place in an earnest and intelligent movement for righteousness in this country

than declamation against the worship of
Baal or Ashteroth. The result of war if
the combatants are otherwsie equally
matched will depend chiefly upon which
Power has prepared best in time of peace.
It is folly for this nation to base any hope
of securing peace on any international
agreement as to the limitation of armaments. We should this year provide for
four battleships. Moreover, the only way
to find out our actual needs is to perform
in time of peace the maneuvers necessary
in time of war. After war is declared
it is too late to find out the needs. [Such
delay] means to invite disaster."

In a special message to Congress the
following April I, again, urged the building of four battleships a year. I con-
tinued:

"It is mischievous folly for any states-
man to assume that this world has yet
reached the stage when a proud nation,
jealous of its honor, can be content to rely
for peace upon the forbearance of other
Powers. Events still fresh in the mind

of every thinking man show that neither arbitration, nor any other device, can as yet be invoked to prevent the gravest and most terrible wrongdoing to peoples who are either few in numbers or who, if numerous, have lost the first and most important of national virtues, the capacity for self defence."

Witness Belgium and China today!

In another message I stated that it would "be criminal to fail to prepare," and in yet another I said:

"The conduct of the Spanish War showed the lamentable loss of life, the useless extravagance and the inefficiency certain to result if during peace the high officers of the War and Navy Departments are praised and rewarded only [for matters against the efficiency of the service]. Money should be appropriated to permit troops to be massed in bodies and exercised in maneuvers, particularly in marching. [I then recommended increases and other measures.] Neglect to provide for all of this means to incur the risk of future disaster and disgrace."

In all these matters I went much further than I could get the Congress to back me up. What I asked for as regards the Navy was proper. As regards the Army, I did not ask for nearly enough, although I went much further than either Congress, or the people behind Congress, were then willing to go. I asked for much more than I got! And it is only just to say that I did get a large response both from Congress and the people, so that by the end of my term the Army had much improved in efficiency, and the Navy had been doubled in size and at least quadrupled in efficiency—at the time when the battle fleet steamed around the world we were easily the second naval power of the world. I felt that I was by my office a leader, that it was the duty of a leader to lead, and that above all it was his duty to lead in the right direction.

If you doubt the need of calling at-

tention to grave shortcomings, let me
ask your attention to what, on this very
day when I am addressing you, has been
said by the Secretaries of War and the
Navy, the President's mouthpieces and
official representatives in dealing with the
entire military policy of the nation, the
most vitally important of all our activities
at this time. The two secretaries, as reported in the New York Tribune, and in
an editorial in the New York Times, have
just denied that there is any shortage in
warm clothing among our troops and sailors, and Mr. Daniels has deprecated
the action of the private individuals who,
separately or associated together, in this
essential matter are endeavoring to make
good the Government's shortcomings by
providing for our troops and sailors the
warm clothing necessary not only to their
comfort but to their health and efficiency
as fighting men. Such denials represent

ignorance pushed to the point of fatuity. They come perilously near representing a wilful and most culpable failure in the performance of one of the most important governmental duties at the present moment.

At the very time that this statement appeared in the press, there also appeared in the press an appeal from our official Red Cross representatives in Paris for a million and a half more sweaters. At that very time all of us who were acquainted with what was happening in at least certain of the training camps knew of widespread discomfort, often rising to suffering, and sometimes to disease and death, due to the failure to provide the raw recruits with the warm clothing essential to health when bitter weather has begun. Scores of officers have written me, or spoken to me, requesting aid in getting overcoats, blankets, jerseys, warm under-

8688

clothes or heavy socks for their men. Scores of men, or relatives of men, have written me asking if I could not do something to remedy the conditions—which I was helpless to remedy. On the morning of the day of my speech I received one letter reading as follows:

"I am in trouble and appeal to you. Enclosed are extracts from my son's letter. He is not a weakling. When only 15 years of age he was driving a six-horse team over some of the worst mountain roads in Idaho. He is a manly man. This letter shows him more concerned for his fellows than himself."

The extract from the letter read:

"Camp So-and-So, Nov. 8, 1917.—The weather has moderated some and we do not suffer so much from the cold. We have no heat in the barracks yet and very few clothes. But for myself I am getting along OK. It is hard on some of the fellows who are sick. The worst of it is we cannot get medical treatment. They have nothing but salts, camly [sic] pills and iodine at the infirmary. So if a man gets sick he is up against it. They are having quite a bit of trouble with contagious diseases such as scarlet fever, measles and spinal meningitis."

A captain from this same camp has just told me that he had one fifth as many overcoats as he had men, and had to use them turn and turn about for the men on guard duty; that he had been able to get thick drawers for the men, but only summer undershirts. A Major-Quartermaster from another camp has just told me that he has at last got plenty of overcoats, but that most of the men still have only cotton uniforms, summer underclothing and light socks. I could multiply these instances indefinitely; they are not exceptional; they stand for the average conditions in at least certain camps. They have been the conditions for nearly three months.

The able officers in the camps are now correcting them; and they would have been corrected far more quickly if there had been outspoken criticism of them.[1]

Now, if those responsible for these conditions had the manliness frankly to acknowledge them, to admit that they, our governmental leaders, had made a capital mistake in the failure to prepare in advance which is chiefly responsible for such conditions, and if with entire disregard of both partisanship and spite our leaders had endeavored to remedy such conditions, I should say not one word about them. I should confine myself to helping remedy

[1] A striking example of the good effects of criticism has just been given by the announcements of the Secretaries of War and the Navy in the papers of day before yesterday to the effect that they now welcome the giving to our soldiers and sailors of warm clothing. Ten days ago, as above recited, they by their public announcements endeavored to discourage all persons from giving such needed clothing to our men (and the Secretary of the Navy, because of a personal quarrel with the Navy League, has refused to let that organization help our sailors in this fashion). The criticism of this action has borne healthy fruit.—*Thanksgiving Day 1917.*

them. But when the conditions are denied, when those responsible for them punish General Wood for having done his high duty in exposing and trying to remedy them, and when these same responsible officials refuse to introduce as our permanent governmental policy the only policy which will prevent the recurrence of these conditions on some occasion when they may bring national ruin, it is unworthy of a patriotic man to keep silent. I believe that we have the finest kind of material in the men, the officers and enlisted men, regulars, volunteers and drafted men alike, who are now gathered in the various training camps. No man can visit these camps, and see these men, without feeling his heart swell with pride as an American. I believe that within a year or so of our entry into the war these men will in spite of all the handicaps have developed into an admirable and formidable army of fighting soldiers. What I wish with all my might to emphasize is that our present experience proves that, in spite of having such excellent natural material, our unpreparedness when we entered the war was so shamefully complete that for a year thereafter we would have been absolutely at the mercy of any formidable opponent, if our Allies had not protected us. I recite the facts in the case only with the hope, the eager hope, that we may take the lesson to heart and so prepare ourselves that never again shall we repeat our folly.

So much for what is really only preliminary to my lecture itself. Now for what I have to say to you students, and therefore to all the other men like you in our nation.

If we cannot look to our college trained men for leadership in our national life, then there is something radically wrong either in the colleges or in the national life. I am not willing to admit that either is the case. Therefore, I confidently appeal to the college men of the United States for practical translation into policy of what in books of advanced theology would be called a proper national ethic and a proper world-ethic. In other words, I ask the men to whom special cultural opportunities have been granted both to teach our people that no nation can help others unless it can defend itself by its own prepared strength, and also to teach them that this strength, the only safe foundation for national greatness, must in international matters be used with high regard for the rights of others.

This is only applying to the nation, in its relation to the world at large, the rule of conduct applicable to the individual within the nation in his relations to other individuals. The man who does not so consult his own interest and the interest of those closest to him as to strive for personal success and achievement is but a poor creature; but if he considers only personal achievement and success, without regard to honesty and to respect for the rights of others, he becomes a noxious jungle beast in the body politic. So it is with nations. China became a source of danger to the peace of the world because it let military inefficiency degenerate into utter military ineptitude. Germany became a worse danger to the peace of the world because it developed the worship of efficiency unbalanced by morality into a monstrous latter-day Moloch-cult. Moreover, Germany, at the same time that she reverted to a world-ethic substantially similar to that of Attila, Genghis Khan and Tamerlane, also made every advance in modern material civilization an efficient aid in the application of this hideous world-ethic.

Of course, the vital thing for the nation no less than the individual to remember is that, while dreaming and talking both have their uses, these uses must chiefly exist in seeing the dream realized and the talk turned into action. It is well that there should be some ideals so high as never to be wholly possible of realization; but unless there is a sincere effort measureably to realize them, glittering talk about them represents merely a kind of self-indulgence which ultimately means atrophy of will power. Ideals that are so lofty as always to be unrealizeable, have a place, sometimes an exceedingly important place, in the history of mankind, if the attempt partially to realize them is made; but in the long run what most helps forward the common run of humanity in this workaday world is the possession of realizeable ideals and the sincere attempt to realize them.

For similar reasons mere closet theorizing about the work of governing or bettering men is only rarely of any use, and is never of as much use as a working hypothesis that is being translated into practice. It is not mere documentation, mere historical or philosophical research, but experimentation, the service test, the test by trial and error, which counts most in the ceaseless struggle for the slow, partial, never very satisfactory, but never-to-be-abandoned uplift of our brother man and sister woman. Robespierre and the other leaders who turned the French revolution from a beneficent movement against one kind of tyrannous injustice into a horrible crusade on behalf of another and even bloodier type of tyrannous injustice, uttered far loftier sentiments, and announced their devotion to far more glittering ideals for all mankind, than Washington and Lincoln ever uttered or announced. But Washington and Lincoln never used lofty words to cloak base actions, never used spangled rhetoric without serious intention to turn it into deeds, never with oratorical insincerity promised what could not be performed, never deliberately pledged themselves to one course of policy and then cynically reversed themselves when it suited their self-interest; and with steady sincerity they carried one consistent purpose to realization in the actual facts of life. Therefore Washington and Lincoln stand at the opposite pole from Robespierre, Danton, Hébert, Marat and their fellow malefactors.

Now, all of these general statements and historical illustrations will probably command the assent of most men of average common sense. I do not expect them to be approved by the persons whose complete refusal to profit by experience, or whose slightly erratic brain development, or whose timidity, make them prefer permanently to dwell in a world of shadows rather than of realities. But most men and women of common sense will not merely agree with them; they will think them too obvious to need elaboration. So they are. But they are by no means too obvious at this moment in so far as reducing them to action is concerned! What we now need—probably what we generally need—in our national life is the reduction to concrete action of that which in the abstract we accept as obvious. The difficulty lies not in securing assent to wisdom as an abstract proposition, but in making men go through the hard, stumbling, painful effort to reduce it to practice.

Therefore, I ask our people, and especially I ask our young men who have been given the boon of university training, to apply these statements to our national conduct during the last three and a half years; to judge our conduct at the present time by the general principles to which we cordially assent as abstract propositions; and then, what is the really important thing, to take steps now, at once, in order that for the future our conduct shall square with the principles which we now see should have been applied in the past.

In putting before ourselves what we, through our Governmental representatives, have done in the past our thought should be only for the future. We recall what is evil in the past, not in order to reproach anyone, but to make sure that it does not recur in the future. After his second election as President, Abraham Lincoln said to a body of men who had come to congratulate him: "Human nature will not change. In any future great national trial, compared with the men of this, we shall have as weak and as strong, as silly and as wise, as bad and as good. Let us therefore study the incidents of this as philosophy to learn wisdom from and none of them as wrongs to be avenged." This is the attitude for us to take now. Whether the acts which have caused the harm were due to silliness or to some even more evil quality, is of no consequence; we do not wish to consider them as anything to be avenged. But we shall ourselves show both silliness and lack of patriotism if we do not learn wisdom from our own shortcomings in the past; and we cannot learn wisdom unless we clearly understand just what these short-comings were, and just what our present position is. It is, of course, entirely true that the faults which are past cannot be repaired, and therefore, so far as this object is concerned, need not be discussed;

but when there is imminent danger of our repeating in the future, when as a matter of fact we are now repeating in the present, these identical faults, it is imperative clearly to realize them, in order to avoid continuance in their commission. We do not wish to cry over spilt milk. But most emphatically we need clearly to understand that it was spilt, and why it was spilt, so as in the future to avoid spilling it when the spilling will be utterly disastrous. As a matter of fact we are still spilling it; and this primarily because we refuse to admit how much we have spilt in the past.

Do you say that there is no need of learning the lesson? If this is your thought, read the daily papers, and study the utterances of our governmental leaders. We have boasted intolerably; we have boasted so much over what we are doing, and over what we intend to do, that we actually tend to forget the one outstanding fact, which is that as yet we have actually done almost nothing.

Remember clearly that the war began just as soon as the Germans sent their submarine note of January 31st last, which we answered by breaking off diplomatic relations on February 3rd. Congress did not declare war in April; it announced that war already existed. And Congress was right. We were exactly as much at war during the two months preceding the action of Congress as during the two months succeeding thereto. If it was inexcusable not to prepare with all possible speed and efficiency after the action in April, it was equally inexcusable not so to prepare immediately after January 31st. The situation had not changed in the smallest degree during the interval. It is now mid November. We are getting towards the close of the tenth month since

Germany has been at war with us (I am using the language of Congress). What have we done during these ten months and how far have our words concealed from ourselves—but from no one else—how little we have done?

Let us consider the last question first. Early in October the Secretary of War issued a couple of statements about the work of the War Department. In one statement he said, as authoritatively quoted in the press: "We are well on the way to the battle front. At the end of another six months, it is safe to predict, the United States will show a record of preparedness and achievement that will challenge the world's admiration." The friendly newspaper giving this statement put in as a headline—"U. S. Will Startle World with Work for War, Says Baker"; and followed the Secretary's statement with this comment, "From a nation of peace and unpreparedness the country in six [by rights eight] months has developed into a powerful fighting machine—the greatest factor in the war. Congress has completed a program which for magnitude and money has no equal in the history of the world's parliaments. . . . On April 6th, the day President Wilson signed the declaration of war, the American army was small and unsupplied. The Navy was not fully manned. America's merchant marine was a joke among nations. The army had less than a dozen aeroplanes." On the previous day the Secretary of War had authorized the statement that "20,000 airplanes are being built for the army," that the country has an "unlimited supply of young men who are being trained for aviators," and that "within a reasonable time, considering the period for preparation, this country will send its first airplane to Europe."

The newspaper in which I saw this statement summarized it by saying that the Secretary had announced that "all these 20,000 airplanes will be completed, with thousands of trained aviators at hand, when Pershing moves to the front." About the same time the oriental investigator and expert of one great paper announced that in view of our having now become a great military nation Japan was hereafter a negligible factor in military affairs and we should forthwith insist on the open door in Manchuria!

These utterances are not exceptional. They are typical. Those which are official are the statements made during a space of two or three days by the gentleman who in war matters speaks for and represents and is responsible for the Administration. The others are the statements of influential newspapers which in good faith accepted what was thus said and built their

theories upon it. In their turn the read-
ers of the newspapers accept both sets of
statements; and relatively well-informed
men hesitate to tell the truth because good
foolish people feel now, as good foolish
people have always felt, that an agreeable
lie is better than a disagreeable truth.

Nothing works graver damage to a nation, especially in war time, than either
dishonest readiness untruthfully to criticise what is right or timid reluctance
truthfully to criticise what is wrong. In
this war the worst and most unpatriotic
action has been that of the men who have
said that we had no special grievance
against Germany and therefore no cause
of war with Germany (if the sinking of
the Lusitania was no special grievance to
this nation then the rape of a woman is
no special grievance to the men who are
her close kin) ; the persons who have op-
posed efficient methods of carrying on the

war; the men who try to escape or help others to escape from rendering military service; and the men who clamor for peace without victory — for an inconclusive peace, which would leave Germany unpunished for her hideous wrongdoing and her vassal states, Austria, Bulgaria and Turkey, still able to oppress the nationalities over which they tyrannize. But second only to these men in the damage they cause, come those other men who deny or seek to cover up the fact that we have been guilty not merely of folly, but of the gravest moral dereliction, in failing to begin to prepare as soon as the great war broke out, that this failure on our part has caused irreparable loss and damage, and that since we entered the war, while we have done some things well, we have done some things very badly.

In the statements above quoted consider first those made officially by the

Secretary of War on behalf of the Administration. They deal in part with what has been done, and in part with prophecy as to what we are going to do. Speaking of what has been done the Secretary of War says "we are well on the way to the battle front." The accuracy of this statement depends upon the standard of speed and accomplishment which we employ in judging such a phrase as "well on the way." After ten months we have failed to reach the battle front, except with one division, which we are informed is in the trenches chiefly for the purpose of instruction; and this means that we have gone towards the front at a snail's pace compared to what every other big nation in the world except China has done and is doing.

We can, if it is any satisfaction, compare ourselves with China. But no other big modern nation for over a hundred

years has been forced after ten months
of war to say only that it was "well on
the way to the front." For comparison
with this kind of military activity we must
go back to the days of Tiglath Pileser,
Nebuchhadnezzar, and Pharaoh Necho.
For the Assyrians and Egyptians of that
period ten months was perhaps not an excessive time in which to begin to prepare
to get "well on the way to the front." But
it is excessive, and more than excessive,
for any nation that realizes that we are
living in the days of the successors of
Moltke. The United States should adopt
the standards of speed in war which be-
long to the 20th Century A. D.; we should
not be content with, still less boast about,
standards which were obsolete in the Sev-
enth Century B. C.

The prophecy following this statement
of achievement is: "At the end of another
six months, it is safe to predict, the United

States will show a record of preparedness and achievement that will challenge the world's admiration."

Perhaps! It depends somewhat upon what the world feels like admiring. But instead of an uneasy hungering to secure the world's admiration without earning it, would it not be well first, without boasting as to what we will do in the future, so to act in the present as to make safe our own self-respect and develop our own assured power of self-reliance, and let the world's admiration take care of itself? It may possibly be true—although I doubt it— that Brag is a good dog; but Holdfast is a better.

As regards airplanes, the Secretary of War announces that we are now preparing 20,000 airplanes and an unlimited supply of aviators. But as regards immediate action he makes only the cautious statement that "within a reasonable time,

considering the period of preparation, this
country will send its first airplane to
Europe." In other words, the 20,000 airplanes with their skilled aviators, trained
in shooting and bomb throwing, are still
in the distance; but our concrete hope is
only that reasonably soon we shall get
one airplane to Europe. I gladly admit
that this is pretty good "considering the
period for preparation." This last is the
essence of the matter. General Squier
and his military and civilian associates,
backed by the big business men engaged
in motor construction and the like, have
done admirably; we have as a nation every
reason to be proud of their energy, ad-
ministrative skill and inventive capacity.
What has been done in the difficult work
of airplane construction has been capital.
But the praise must be limited by the
phrase "considering the period for preparation." The men who have done the

job are not responsible for having been forced to begin two years and three quarters after they ought to have begun. But we as a people, through our high governmental authorities, have no right to excuse ourselves for the almost inconceivable delay in beginning by apologetically "considering the period for preparation." It is purely our fault that the men who are doing the job have had to take into account such a "consideration."

We must also remember that while we are still only beginning to build the twenty thousand airplanes, and beginning to train the future twenty thousand aviators to fly, we have not yet even begun to train the few hundred aviators we already have, to fight. After the best type of airplane has been produced in vast numbers, and after the tens of thousands of men necessary have been trained to handle them in the air, it will still be necessary to train them how to do the actual shooting against the war-hawks on the other side, and the actual bombing at the same time that they dodge the anti-aircraft guns of the enemy. We have waited to learn all this and to do all this until war actually came, although for over two years and a half we were vouchsafed such warning as no other nation in recent times has had in advance of war. We are now able to do all this, we now have the necessary year or eighteen months in which to build machines and train men, only because the weary and war worn allies, to whose help we have nominally come, deem it worth while, for their own sakes, to protect us with their fleets and armies, with the bodies of their bravest and the brains of their wisest, while we at last do what it was unpardonable for us not to have done long in advance.

Why cry over spilt milk you say? Because now is the time to provide that it shall not be spilt in the future; and we never shall so provide if we complacently ignore the fact that it has been spilt in the past. Remember that we have not yet taken one step to make preparedness our permanent policy. On the contrary, our leaders vaguely hold out the hope that we can avoid such a policy by devising some patent fake policy of permanent pacifism after the war. To rely on any policy of pacifism as a substitute for (instead of, as I would gladly admit it to be, an addition and supplement to) the policy of training and preparing in advance our national strength, would be criminal. And the only sure way of averting the introduction of a foolish pacifist policy is by profiting by the humiliating experience through which we are now going, and introducing now, immediately, the policy of real preparedness as a permanent feature of our governmental action.

So much for the governmental announcements. Now for the newspaper statements based on these governmental announcements. Remember that these newspaper statements come from high grade, reputable papers, sincerely bent on telling the truth; but apparently completely misled as to the real facts, and apparently not in a position to understand what time means in preparation for modern warfare. One statement is that "the country has developed into a powerful fighting machine—the greatest factor in the war." This is a translation of rose-tinted prophecy into exactly what it is not—the sobriety of accomplished fact. We have not developed into a "powerful fighting machine." On the contrary, after nearly ten months we are such a weak fighting machine that we have not yet put men, guns or airplanes on the permanent fighting line. To speak of a "powerful fighting machine" which after ten months isn't ready to do any fighting, is a ludicrous contradiction in terms.

It is even more ludicrous—and humiliating—to speak of our being "the greatest factor in the war." Why, the German authorities regarded us, and still regard us, with such contempt that they counted our entire warlike might as of less consequence than the liberty to go on with their U-boat warfare. As yet, either France or England is a tenfold—a hundredfold—greater factor in the war than the United States. Von Tirpitz has just said that "from a military standpoint America's entrance into the war is of little significance." And boasts do not aid us. They are hurtful to our self-respect. They tend to do positive damage by encouraging a

silly complacency. Consider the headline
above quoted: "The United States will
startle world with work for war." This
may, or may not, prove true in the future;
at present so much of the world as
is represented by Von Tirpitz and
Von Hindenburg has certainly not been
startled to edification or admiration by
our leisurely "work for war." And it is
on the basis of this imaginary achievement
that one facile adviser proposes that we
shall embark on a career of pointless inter-
ference in Manchuria—as an addition to
the war in which we are already engaged,
and to the simmering trouble in Mexico,
so full of future menace.

But there were certain of these newspaper statements which were absolutely
true, although the full significance of their
truth had escaped the writers. It is absolutely true that Congress, with wise gen-
erosity in endeavoring to help the Admin-

istration atone for our appalling blunder
in failing to prepare in advance, has appropriated money in huge sums, vaster
than ever before appropriated by any
legislature in the world. It is also lamentably true that on April 6th, when we at
last formally admitted the obvious truth
that we were already at war (and when
we had been for two years and eight
months constantly warned as hardly another nation in history has ever been
warned), the navy was not fully manned,
the army was small and unsupplied, there
were less than a dozen military airplanes
(which incidentally were worthless for
military purposes) and the American
merchant marine was a joke among nations.

All this is absolutely true. But is it a
subject of congratulation? The money
appropriated represents at least twice—
it is alleged to be three times—what Eng-

land has spent in any year of the war. It is certainly twice what would have been necessary to spend if we had started to get ready in time. In such case there would have been no need for the frantic hurry and reckless prodigality which our culpable refusal to exercise forethought has rendered necessary. From the mere standpoint of economy, even aside from the more important standpoint of trained efficiency, we have already paid an overwhelming money price for our almost inconceivable blindness in the face of the lesson which for over three years has been written in letters of blood and flame across the whole world-horizon.

We have not yet paid that price in blood; and the reason is that our allies have paid it for us. For their own sakes our people should clearly understand how great our failure in duty has been, how completely we owe our salvation to others,

and how little we have a right to hope
ever again to escape scatheless unless we
learn wisdom and prepare so that never
again shall there be such failure. It is a
continuing failure. We are not yet doing
our duty. This is of course largely due to
the fact that it is impossible after three
years indulgence in folly not to continue
to pay for that folly. But it is in part
also due to the fact that our refusal fear-
lessly to admit and condemn the folly of
the past has fearfully handicapped us in
the effort to avoid the commission of folly
in the present.

The men who clamored against preparedness before the war played Germany's game, and wrought irreparable
evil to this country and to mankind; for
if we had prepared our strength in advance, and had acted with instant efficiency when our own wrongs became intolerable, Russia would not have broken,

nor Italy have met disaster, and the peace
of victory would have come to us long ago
—perhaps even without our having had
to fight at all. The heads of organizations such as the German-American Alli-
ances which acted frankly in the interest of Germany were no worse foes
than the various organizations of professional pacifists and the like, so far as
preparedness was concerned. The agents
of the German Government used all
these bodies of people, just as they
used the socialists and the I. W. W.
These allies and agents of Germany now
oppose sending our troops abroad, oppose
the Liberty loans, and denounce every action taken by the Government against our
domestic traitors. These men are against
the government when it does right. They
are worse, but they are only one degree
worse, than the sheep-like creatures—
often misled by very sinister creatures—

who bleat the ignoble doctrine that we must "stand behind" the government, with blinded eyes, even when it does wrong. The men who take the latter attitude, however feebly good their intentions, are as a matter of fact largely responsible for what we as a people have done that was bad; for by their tame acquiescence in evil actions and evil policies and by their antagonism to their more fearless fellow citizens who honestly tell the truth, they have put a premium on inefficiency, and on even graver shortcomings. Every American worth his salt should in every way aid the Government in every measure to wage the war efficiently, and to get our whole weight into the war with the utmost speed; and he should also make it clear that he will not tolerate or condone delay, inefficiency, irresolution or failure in single-minded patriotism.

For two years and a half we failed in

any way to prepare for the tremendous war which—as should have been obvious to even the most frivolous and timid—might at any moment suck us into the maelstrom. We made no effort even to do such an elementary thing as to run the Government rifle factories full speed. We passed a vicious law which impaired the efficiency of the national guard—a volunteer organization—and interfered with the development of other efficient volunteer organizations. We treated the proper organization of the War and Navy Departments, from the heads down, as a matter not merely for indifference but for levity. We turned not merely the other cheek but our whole person to the brutal German aggressor, and showed such fear of standing up either for our own rights or for the rights of small well-behaved nations, that we put a premium on increasing brutality of aggression.

Then on January 31st last Germany notified us that she would conduct her submarine warfare with absolute ruthlessness —in other words, that she spurned our warning because she felt utter contempt for our soft and unready strength, that she was convinced of the efficacy of the policy of schrechlichkeit, that she regarded the damage she could do her enemies by U-boat warfare as outweighing any possible effect of the hostility of the United States.

When we went into the war General Von Hindenburg was reported in the public press as saying that he saw no need for Germany to fear anything America might do for eighteen months. We scoffed at the statement. But nearly ten months have gone by, and most certainly we have as yet given Germany scant cause for fear. The country was utterly unprepared for war; the War Department was

utterly unprepared for war; and the
army, taken as a whole, was badly prepared for war. Perhaps in no way was
our spiritual unpreparedness more clearly
shown than in our failure to comprehend
the tremendous importance of time; and
this although the last three years had
shown again and again that time in modern war is a vital factor. Germany has
counted on our delays. Germany was
justified. We have certainly so far failed
to show any appreciation of the fact that
in modern war, and in preparation for
modern war, time is more valuable than
ever it was or is in business.

Nearly ten months have passed. We
have but one division fit to go into the
trenches. During the century that elapsed
between Waterloo and the invasion of
Belgium the average war between great
military powers lasted much less than this
time. It is not a figurative or hyperbolic

statement, it is the literal truth that during these ten months any one of the great military powers could have conquered us with but little more difficulty than was experienced in the conquest of Belgium, Servia or Roumania. We have owed our safety solely to the fact that for their own purposes it suited England and France to protect us behind the rampart of their gallant dead. Are the descendants of the Americans of the Revolution and the Civil War to be permanently content with such precarious and ignoble safety?

Above all, are they much longer to submit to the treacherous wrong done this Republic by the Hearsts and La Follettes who have directly or indirectly preached an evil hatred of those very Allies to whom we owe our safety? There is even a lower depth than that plumbed by the men who would sacrifice this country to their love of Germany; and this depth is plumbed by those who whether from sheer sinister malice or from demagogic desire to pander to that malice would sacrifice this country to their hatred of England.

Late in the tenth month since Germany went to war with us we have near the front one division of infantry, entirely fit to fight. There are some regiments of engineers also fit for work on the fighting front. There are some regiments of artillery which have learned their business with French guns, and which are doubtless fit. We have some other divisions which are rapidly becoming fit. We have as yet no battle planes, and no airmen fit for battle work in the sense that the German, French and English war-hawks (including the Americans in the French air squadrons) are fit. After so many months of immense money expenditure and great, although often misdirected, effort, this nation of a hundred million people, the wealthiest in the world, which prides itself on its energy, has not yet produced an army, fit to meet the enemy, which is as large or as efficient as the small armies which the wrecked remnant of either Servia, Roumania or Belgium has in the field. Is this a satisfactory showing?

When such is the actual lesson of the results of unpreparedness, are we still to admit that there is any patriotism, any genuine love of country, among the pacifist creatures who now clamor against the war, or among the politicians who still refuse to introduce preparedness as our permanent military policy, and who still talk vaguely about future international agreements, which they assert will hereafter save us from war by scraps of paper instead of by our own trained strength? Keep clearly in mind what our purpose is. I am not primarily concerned with the

mistakes and shortcomings actually committed by us during these ten months; I
comment on these only when the effort is
made to deny their existence. But I am
vitally concerned with seeing us as a people learn aright the lesson of the far
reaching evil caused by our complete
failure to prepare during the two years
and three quarters preceding April last.
Every shortcoming of which we have been
guilty, every avoidable disaster that has
befallen or will befall us or our allies, is
or will be due primarily to our failure to
prepare in advance. Unless we clearly
see and manfully acknowledge this fact
we shall not learn a correct policy, and
unless we alter our present policy, ruin
will in the end surely be our children's
portion.

At home our army has been gathered
together in great camps, which have for
the most part been admirably constructed.

The regulars and the volunteer regiments, consist three fourths—in many cases almost entirely — of raw recruits. The drafted men, excellent material, whose spirit of fine patriotism is beyond praise, have been or are being gathered together; for weeks most of them either had no arms or only broomsticks; and now they have rifles, mostly obsolete Spanish-war rifles, in the proportion of about one rifle for every six or eight men finally to be gathered in each camp. There has been no target practice. Most of the guns in the artillery regiments are of wood. Many thousands—I am informed that in certain camps nearly all—of the men, in this cold weather, still have cotton uniforms, or thin summer underclothes, or an insufficient number of overcoats. It is only by chance that we hear of what has gone wrong (the Germans are fully advised—it is only our people who are ignorant—and the men who shiver in thin cotton or drill with cordwood cannon are not ignorant). But the press has from time to time mentioned the fact that many of the cartridges turned out are defective; that scores of millions of the primers have turned out to be worthless.

It has been jauntily said that the shortage of rifles among the troops who are in training is of no consequence, that men can at first learn with broomsticks, and that the eight men allotted to each antiquated rifle can drill, turn and turn about, with it. These statements are not in accordance with the facts. Competent officers, engaged in training troops of good capacity, know that each man should be given his rifle, and should be learning to keep it clean and to take pride in it, within a week. If the officer is very good, and the man also good, the rifle ought to be given the latter on the second or third

day—or even on the first. The Platts-
burg men were given their rifles after a
couple of days. In 1898 the men of my
regiment were given their rifles as soon
as they arrived at camp. Colonel Leon-
ard Wood, now Major General Wood,
who was in command of the regiment, pro-
ceeded on the theory that every single
thing should be done at the earliest possible moment; and that if anything whatever
could be done at three o'clock and wasn't
done until four o'clock, somebody was to
be blamed and should be called to account.
In consequence that regiment was armed,
equipped, drilled, kept two weeks on
transports and put through two victorious
aggressive fights, in which it lost a third
of its officers and a fifth of its men, within
ninety days of the time the Colonel and
Lieutenant Colonel received their com-
missions. English and Canadian officers
of high rank have told me that under in-

tensive training they have been able to put thousands of men in the field within sixteen weeks.

Probably our gravest shortcoming after Germany in effect declared war on us on January 31st last was our failure instantly and with all possible speed to begin the preparation of a giant fleet of cargo ships, at the same moment that we undertook the investigation of the U-boat problem. The German government accepted war with us rather than give up the indiscriminate submarine campaign of murder and destruction. In other words, it announced that in its view the vital feature of the war was the effort to destroy so much of the shipping of the world as would hamper the transport of men, food and munitions until England was brought to her knees. Germany knew the value of time. She began her campaign without one hour's delay. She counted on our indecision, folly and timidity to make us delay. And she was right. It seems literally incredible that we should have let one hour pass after the receipt of Germany's challenge before bending our every effort towards the immediate large-scale production of swift cargo ships. Yet for three months nothing was done, and then three months were wasted by permitting a squabble in the interest of worthless wooden shipping—and of Germany!—to block all preparation. Six months were wasted in utter futility before any serious attempt was made to grapple with the gravest feature of the war situation; and this although for two years we had been intermittently threatening and blustering (and backing down) about this very matter, and had finally gone to war about it; so that by no human possibility could we have had clearer and more emphatic and more often reiterated warning.

In a war in which it has been shown again and again that a difference of a week or two—almost of a day or two—in readiness may mark the difference between overwhelming victory and measureless disaster, we have acted as if months of hesitation and leisurely discussion were of negligible consequence. In some particular bureaus there has been full realization of the vital importance of speed. But as a rule we have in practice adopted the view of a high official who recently spoke of a delay of two or three months, as a "perfectly endurable delay." Why, a single day's delay ought to be treated as unendurable if we really mean to do our utmost.

Our Allies get money from us and need more; they sadly need our aid; and they are bound to speak with the utmost politeness of all our shortcomings and failures. But let us make no mistake. It is only

by so acting as to win our own self-respect
that we can permanently win the respect
of others, whether friends or foes; and we
jeopardize everything by inefficiency and
procrastination, and by foolish reluctance
to face the fact that there has been inefficiency and procrastination. Fine words
will not permanently cloak either ugly
deeds or the absence of deeds. Prodigal
expenditure of money and large ship-
ments of food will not atone for the failure speedily to put great masses of trained
fighting men on the battle front. Uncle
Sam must show that he is a soldier and
not a sutler. To do a thing six months
after it should have been done may represent complete failure, and cannot represent complete success. Nine tenths of wisdom is being wise in time.

We have been able to prepare at all,
we have been able to waste time in discussion and hesitating and blundering,

only because it was worth while for our allies to protect our unhardened, unready softness of bulk with their own hardened strength.   But let us not prattle about "perfectly endurable delay"! If our allies had not, for their own purposes, shielded us, our frightened citizens would now be doing the bidding of stern and brutal men in pickel-haubes. Our allies have protected us; we have not paid in blood for our protection; but the blood of our allies has paid for our safety. Every month of what was to us "perfectly endurable delay," has been paid for by them in the blood of a hundred thousand men. No man can tell how much our delay has cost. By beginning to act with energy on February 1st, the day after the German note arrived, we could have had hundreds of thousands of efficient fighting men at the front in August; and in such event it may well be that Russia would have taken heart and would now be organized for self-respecting, orderly liberty and for victory, and that Italy (especially if we had done our clear duty by declaring war on Austria) would not have met with disaster. Of course, if we had obeyed the dictates of ordinary common sense, foresight and patriotism and had begun to prepare three years ago—in men, machines and ships—we could have put a couple of million men into the field last April and the war would be over now; or rather it would in all probability have come to an end without further bloodshed the instant we decided to interfere, so that we would not actually have had to fight.

The lesson of the vital need of preparedness in advance is the vital lesson for us to learn. I ask you to remember that I am trying to make us, the people as a whole, learn this lesson; I wish us to learn from our own shortcomings; I wish

us to take home the lesson to ourselves,
to the American people, and not to make
believe that it should only be learned by
our officials or by somebody else. I care
not a rap for the politics of those who
need to learn the lesson. The extracts
from my speeches and writings above
given show that I have preached this lesson just as freely when the individuals
affected belonged to my own party as
when they belonged to another party.

Let our people learn aright the lesson
taught by the last three years. We refused to prepare. We followed the foolish prophets of pacifism when with quavering voices they told us that if we were
only harmless enough nobody would hurt
us, and that preparedness brought on war.
We tried the experiment. We did not
prepare. And we have the war. Unpreparedness did not avert war. It merely
rendered us helpless to do our part worth-

ily during a period so long that if it had not been for our allies we would have been conquered twice over. Preparedness generally, although not always, averts war. Unpreparedness always invites it, and usually ensures disaster.

The other day the public press carried this statement:

"Washington, October 5th.—Frank admission by Senator James Hamilton Lewis that the United States was not prepared to meet the exigency of war when five months ago it found itself confronted with an actual state of hostilities was made on the floor of the Senate today in a speech in which the Illinoisan endeavored to answer the recent Roosevelt charge that our preparedness was 'broomstick preparedness.' The Senator said:

" 'There may be something to be said in justification of the fact that we were not prepared to the extent that we should have been. It was because we were a people dedicated to peace. It was because the mothers of the land prayed that the nation should ever be consecrated to peace.' "

This puts the case for unpreparedness in a nutshell; and the commentary on this theory, upon which for two years and a half we acted, is furnished by what befell us at the end of those two and a half years. If our people cannot learn the lesson thus taught, and if we ever again incline to the teachings of the pacifists, then indeed we shall surely be brayed in a mortar before our folly depart from us. Undoubtedly before we went into this war there were plenty of women, and just about the same number of men, of the ostrich type who believed that if they hid their heads so that they could not see war it would not come. Many of them were good, intelligent people who had never been taught unpleasant international truths and who were cruelly wronged by astute and unconscientious leadership in high places. Many were simply fatuous. They "prayed that the nation might ever be dedicated to peace" and did not realize that the prayer could be made effective only if they at the same time made ready against war. They had forgotten one half of the old Cromwellian adage: "Trust in the Lord and keep your powder dry!" They bleated a make-believe trust; and they let the powder grow wet. Those "mothers of the land" who were fit to be the spiritual heirs of the women of the Revolution and the Civil War, had raised their sons to be soldiers for the right, to put justice before peace, and to be proudly ready to give everything, life itself, when the nation needed the sacrifice. The other poor mothers, less farsighted or less wise, who took the attitude Senator Lewis describes, and the men who were their fitting mates, with quavering timidity refused to do the only thing that might avert war; and now the war has come anyhow, and their boys, untrained in soul and body, are in the draft army—where, thank Heaven, they will be trained, where they will stand beside the other boys who were raised to be soldiers for the right, and out of which they will be turned as up-standing, self-respecting American citizens, with neither a spiritual nor a physical stoop in the shoulders, and able to look the whole world straight in the eyes without flinching.

We are a nation of tremendous potential strength. We cannot now by any possible exertion utilize more than a small fraction of that strength until after over a year from the time when we were dragged into the war. And even in this belated fashion we cannot use that strength with full efficiency unless we clearly understand the lamentable harm we have done by refusing to harden it or make it useful during these fateful years. Our shortcomings and needs leap to the eye when we compare ourselves with certain small commonwealths. Portugal, one year after going to war, put (by transport over the ocean) 75,000 trained soldiers at the front. This is as if in February we put a million and a half fighting men into the firing line. To do relatively as much as Canada and Australia have done we ought to put five million men under arms. Some of our advocates — and exponents — of delay have stated that the English took two years and a half before making their land forces efficient in this war. In the first place the statement is untrue; after a year and a half the British Army became a formidable fighting machine. In the next place, the argument amounts to saying that we should refuse to profit by the mistakes of the British, and should repeat them all over—and amplify them—on our own account. Finally, these soft apologists of inefficiency forget that the British during the year and a half before their army became relatively as efficient as the armies of the Germans and the French, nevertheless bore a constantly increasing share of the burden. Within the first three months of the war they had placed over two hundred thousand men in the thick of the hardest fighting; steadily they increased the numbers, more than making good the awful losses; steadily they improved guns and men, using at first (because of lack of shells—and of training) double the number of men for a given frontage that the French used; *but using them, and constantly extending their share of the line, and thus relieving the*

hard-pressed French. If during the first
ten months of the war England had done
as little as we have done in the past ten
months, gallant France would surely have
broken. If she had prepared her strength
after war broke out in as leisurely a man-
ner as we have done, the war would now
be over and Germany enthroned as world-
victor.

Our business is to exert the largest possible fraction of our strength at the earliest possible moment, and then to exert our
constantly growing strength as fast as
with the utmost energy and efficiency we
can develop it, until we win the peace of
overwhelming victory. This war, as far
as we are concerned, was brought on by
German militarism and American pacifism
working together. To let either or both
of them dictate the peace that is to end it
would be an immeasureable disaster. We
should not have any negotiations with

those who committed and who glory in the Lusitania infamy, the rape of Belgium, and the hideous devastation and wholesale murders and slavery in the conquered countries; and the Hearsts and La Follettes and Germanized Socialists and I. W. W. and Pacifist leaders who advocate such negotiations are the enemies of this nation and of all mankind. We are fighting for the fundamental sanctities of life and decencies of civilization. We are fighting for the liberty of every well behaved nation, great or small, to have whatever government it desires and to live unharming others and unharmed by others. We are sending our troops to fight abroad so that they may not have to fight at home. Germany must be beaten, and the Prussianized militaristic autocracy of the Hohenzollerns humbled or the world will not be safe for liberty-loving peoples. We must fight this war through to victory no matter what the cost in time or money or in the blood of our bravest and dearest.

And on this point again let us always insist that our rulers do not shame us and weaken our moral fibre by loose rhetoric, but speak only when they have pondered their words, and make good the words when once spoken. In actual fact we entered the war only because we had a special grievance against Germany, a grievance of so grave a character that we exposed ourselves to humiliation, we were guilty of a tame lack of self-respect, when we did not go to war two years earlier; for when the Lusitania was sunk we should have acted as we did finally act last February; in the intervening two years there had been no change in the situation; indeed our condonation of the Lusitania's sinking had put us in a slightly worse position—and unquestionably our

people would have been more united, and
more heartily ready to back the war, if
we had acted with instant and resolute
courage at the time of the great tragedy.
When once we did act, and entered the
war, we became committed to our Allies,
and any man who has since assailed any
one of them, or defended Germany, or
sought an inconclusive peace is a traitor
to this country. Our grievance against
Germany was not merely special but
ample and intolerable. A few weeks
later, however, we announced that our
purpose was to make the world safe for
democracy. Unless this statement was a
piece of mere empty magniloquence, of
highfalutin' rhetoric, it pledged us to immense sacrifice in a hard, dangerous crusade, eminently righteous but for an object in which our own concern was slight.
Personally, I was and am eagerly ready
to enter into such a crusade, if our people

seriously intend to put it through; but our people ought thoroughly to understand what it means. We were not bound to enter on it. Our grievance was against Germany, and we could with honor have joined with our allies to war against her until she was overthrown, and then make peace in such fashion as to guarantee justice to them and to us, and to make the world a little safer for all of us in consequence. But a pledge to "make the world safe for democracy" is a solemn engagement to smash the two nations which most conspicuously make democracy unsafe within their own borders—Austria and Turkey (and to punish Bulgaria is a necessary incident thereto). Any peace which leaves Turkey in Europe, and which leaves the Armenians, the Syrian Christians, the Jews and the Arabs under Turkish rule, conspicuously fails to make the world safe for democracy—or, for liberty and decency; Germany is a danger to her neighbors; but the Poles, Danes and Frenchmen or men with French hearts over whom she tyrannizes are numerically only a fraction as numerous as the mass of men of different races to whom liberty is denied by the dual tyranny of the Germans and Magyars of Austria-Hungary. I speak with no bitterness towards either the Austrian Germans or the Hungarian Magyars; I would protest against seeing any other race tyrannize over them; I merely wish that they shall tyrannize over no one else. Until within a very few years of the outbreak of this war, I had hoped for Austria a great future—especially during the long period when the internal condition of Servia made it seem hopeless to look to her as a regenerative influence in the Balkan Peninsula. I had hoped that Austria would solve the exceedingly complex and difficult situation of southwestern Europe by developing into a great federal commonwealth, in which the German, the Magyar, the Pole, the Czech-Slovak, the Rouman, the Jugo-Slav, and perhaps others, might join; each sovereign within his own linguistically and ethnically rounded out and self-governing state; but all united under one rule which should keep the peace among these different states, and should use their common strength to forbid aggression against them from without. I had hoped this when Bosnia and Herzegovina were taken by Austria; it seemed as if such a policy of federation on a footing of just equality opened the way for a great and unique career to Austria; the heir apparent whose assassination was the occasion (not the cause) of this war was reputed to hold such views; and I gave them up with unfeigned reluctance, and only when it was

evident that they were no longer tenable.
This war has shown that Austria has become a subject-ally of Germany and an
enemy of freedom and civilization. Unless we resolutely intend to break up both
Austria and Turkey, and insist on liberty
for the subject races in the two countries,
our talk about "making the world safe
for democracy" is a sham.

People forget very easily, and it is hard
for them to learn even the plainest lessons
from history. There have been of recent
years, and still are, certain forces at work
among us which ominously resemble certain of the forces which worked to ruin
France at the end of the Empire of Napo-
leon the Third. In De La Gorce's exceedingly able, delightfully written, and
sombre History of the Second Empire,
there is a very vivid account of the French
mental attitude at the time of the Exposition of 1867. This Exposition was loudly

heralded as ushering in an era of permanent international peace; and the materialists, the pacifists, the sordid profiteers, and the wild demagogues and doctrinaire reformers all joined in saying that there was to be thereafter no danger of international wars, and that everybody need think only of money, and enjoyment, and of two kinds of indulgence—indulgence in more or less gross bodily pleasure, and, as an antidote, indulgence in a more or less unhealthy sentimentality. Then, just as the hard money getters, and the gay pleasure lovers, and the foolish sentimentalists had all determined to live on the theory that serious war was a danger of the past, came the notice, from those best competent to judge, that the country must prepare to defend itself against the military power of others. Says La Gorce: (I condense and translate freely)—"The shock was equally great to the lovers of material pleasure, to the dreamers of universal peace [this was just fifty years ago —how often war has come since!] and to the credulous optimists who with easy faith had accepted the theories of the Government. . . . The statement that 'the influence of a nation depends upon the number of men it can put under arms' sounded repulsively material to an intelligent people dreaming of the fraternity of nations and of perpetual peace. The sentimental humanitarianism preached by the Government had been accepted by the rank and file of the people; and now, when the Government had turned round, the people had only to recall its former teachings in order to justify resistance of its new precepts. The love of easy living, the weakening of the sense of collective duty, had made the idea of self-sacrifice very unpleasant. The old martinets of the regular army refused to believe that there was anything wrong with that army. Critics of what had been done were told that it was unbecoming publicly to expose the shortcomings of the Government, lest the enemies of the country be encouraged, and the faith of the people disturbed. Congressmen who were desirous to placate their constituents made much of the National Guard; [only a very few leaders] spoke with sincerity and foresight, warning their fellow country-men that great wars in the future were inevitable, and that it was well to be wise and ready before the event and not after it. The Legislators and their constituents were to blame for refusing to take account of future perils; but the principal responsibility rested on the [Executive] Government, to which the people had submitted in a spasm of servile obedience while it led them wrong but which they followed partially and doubtfully when late in the day it turned to the path of wisdom."

Surely there are unpleasant analogies between what is thus described, and what we have of recent years seen in our own country. Surely, the same overwhelming disaster would have befallen us this year that overwhelmed France nearly half a century ago, had not we, more fortunate than the France of 1870, found our folly and weakness at least temporarily protected by the fleets and armies of other nations. Let us profit by the lesson; and while we thankfully accept the fact that others have saved us from the punishment for unwisdom, let us beware of misreading the lesson; and the only way by which to show that we have read it aright, is to show by our actions that never again will we be caught in such a condition of complete unpreparedness, of unreadiness and inability to do our duty by ourselves and by others.

The young Americans like those I am

addressing owe to their country the duty
of leadership; and this leadership is
needed both for our immediate task and
our ultimate task. The immediate task
is to win this war. All our immediate
energies ought now to be bent towards
this end. We must accept no peace except the peace of overwhelming triumph.
The energy and business efficiency and
individual courage and self-reliance which
are among our national traits are slowly
enabling us to overcome the frightful
handicap created by our refusal to prepare during the two and a half years before we drifted into the war. During the
last ten months we have not done a half
or a quarter of what we could have done.
But even the exertion of a half or a quarter of our giant strength will by the end
of a year produce good results. There is
now reason to hope that within a year or
so of the time when we entered the war—

that is, by the end of the winter, or in the
early spring of 1918—we shall be able to
begin seriously to fight instead of merely
paying others to fight for us, and that we
shall become a ponderable element in the
war. Six months later we ought to have
begun to be one of the great factors in the
war. We can be sure that our armies at
the front and that our fleets and squadrons will do well and bravely, and that we
shall hold our heads high because of their
valor. Theirs is the great task, theirs will
be the great glory. Let us who stay behind back them in every way!

The ultimate task of the young men of
today of the type of those whom I address, is so to lead the generation now
coming on the stage that this nation shall
assure its international safety by grasping
and acting on the fundamentals of duty.
Most certainly the nation can be redeemed
from mere gross, self-indulgent material-

ism and from the silly, sham-sentimentality which so often goes hand in hand with materialism. I sincerely believe that on the whole we of this nation have a little finer material on which to work than is true of any other nation; that in our land there are on the whole better ideals than elsewhere of the duty of man and woman to one another, to their neighbors, to their country, and to the world at large. I do not see how any man can go through the camps where our army is now being trained without feeling a thrill of pride in the manliness, energy and resourcefulness of the men who are there slowly acquiring not only the bodies of soldiers but the feelings of patriots. Those camps are today the great universities of American citizenship, and we ought to make them permanent features of our national life. There could be no finer material for citizenship than that afforded by the men and women of this nation; and all the greater will be our reproach if we permit it to be wasted or warped out of shape.

I am not here discussing those qualities of personal and social morality which stand as basic in all healthy national life. At the moment I am only asking you for such leadership in our public affairs as shall make this nation spiritually and physically ready and eager both to do full and generous justice to others and also to secure justice from others, and especially from the strong. This nation must be able to develop within itself such powers as will in turn make it able to defend itself from all outside aggression, and also make it able, with some modicum of success, to work toward making things a little better in the international world. And there must be at least an approximation to strength and justice in our own internal dealings or we shall assuredly, when the crisis comes, lack the power to defend ourselves against any formidable outside enemy.

If our people refuse to profit by the teachings of history, let them at any rate learn by what is now happening in the world, before their eyes. The case of Russia is full of melancholy instruction for us, if only we refuse to treat it as having happened in another firmament. Let us translate what has occurred into the terms of reaction and of semi-revolutionary folly which apply in our own country; and you men of University training should throw your whole strength equally against both the foolish or sinister representatives of reaction who invite and justify revolution, and the foolish or sinister apostles of revolution who invite and justify reaction.

With us the reactionaries are the men, and above all the very wealthy men, who

permit the maxims of an outward indus-
trial creed to blind them to the need that
we shall be our brother's keepers to the
extent not only of securing him full justice but of training him aright, lest he lay
hands on the pillars of the temple of civilization and bring the whole structure
toppling down to bury both him and us.
The selfish reactionaries of business and
politics, whether great or small, if they
had their way unchecked would invite the
fate that the Tsar's bureaucracy brought
on Russia.

And in Russia, on the morrow after the
forces of despotism were overthrown, the
forces of anarchy and disorder, under the
leadership of demagogues and sinister or
impractical doctrinaires, became the worst
foes of liberty and democracy. So it is
here. The Hearsts and La Follettes and
Stones and Bergers and Hillquits, the
agitators of the I. W. W. and the Ger-

manized-American socialists, are of precisely the same type as the men who seek to tear free Russia to pieces, whose excesses and follies have thrown great tracts of her territory under the feet of the German aggressor, and who continuously threaten either to render her a byword of failure or else to re-enthrone some form of the old tyranny. Let us shun as we would shun the plague, both the White Terror of reaction and the Red Terror of revolution. France was brought to disaster by the tyranny of the Old Regime; and then again by the Robespierres, Dantons, Héberts and Marats, whose wickedness almost eclipsed that of the most evil of their royal predecessors. The extremists of reaction and the extremists of revolution play into one another's hands; and all men of courage, patriotism and foresight must war with equal energy against both, under penalty of being false to the cause of orderly liberty, alike in this Republic and in the world at large.

Justice at home must be the basis of our strength. But justice is not enough. On it we must build the strength, else the justice will vanish before alien aggression. A nation of freemen can only remain free if the freemen in time of peace train themselves to defend their freedom in war. There is no title to the enjoyment of a right which is not properly based upon the performance of a duty, and the fundamental national duty is the duty of self-defence just as the fundamental political right is the suffrage. Universal suffrage should be based on universal service. A cardinal feature of the permanent policy of this liberty-loving democratic Republic should be the acceptance of the principle of universal obligatory military training and military service for all our young men.